Across the Line
by
Anthony Brough
ISBN: 978-1-914933-64-6

"One day I will find the right words, and they will be simple"

Jack Keruoac, The Dharma Bums.

Dedication

For Mike and Kath Brough, who showed me the value
of hard work and great literature.

Introduction

Hi, thank you for taking the time to open my first book of poetry, *Across the Line*. My name is Tony Brough, and these poems are my reflections on life as I reach fifty-five, a significant birthday in a number of respects.

It's long been my ambition to publish a book; I finished a novel at the age of thirty and promptly realised it was a mess. The novel went in the bin, my ambition placed on a dusty shelf at the back of my brain, and life moved on. When all our lives stopped moving in early Spring 2020, however, I decided to dust off the idea of writing a book, although this time a book of poetry. These fifty-five poems are an attempt to tell a story that I feel is often untold, although no doubt familiar to a great many people: I wanted to articulate the life experiences of a working-class lad brought up in the 1970s and 1980s. For the past twenty-eight years I have had the privilege of teaching History for a living. I've basically been paid to tell stories, so this book is an attempt to tell a more personal historical story in a (hopefully) readable style.

I was born in Gatley, Cheshire, in February 1968, in my Grandparent's house. I then lived in Singapore for eighteen months before moving back to Britain, this time to Cheadle. These days, Cheshire is synonymous with posh, but that wasn't the case in the 1970s. Both my parents' and grandparents' houses were council built and council owned, however Thatcher hadn't yet stigmatised and sold off council housing during my childhood, and where I grew up was lovely. Most of my mates came from my estate; all of our parents worked, although nobody really knew what anybody else's parents did for a living. Our lives had a duality to it that, to be honest, affects me to this day. From the date the clocks sprang forward to the day they fell backwards, we lived outdoors. We had playing fields directly behind our house, and just over the road as well. The field behind our house was bordered on one side by the length of our road and on the other by the Micker Brook. If we weren't playing cricket or football on the 'rec' (the field in front) we were messing around near the river, on rope swings or building rafts from supplies we had pilfered from the Industrial estate at the end of our road; we were neither angels nor devils. Then winter hit, and as laissez-faire as parents often were during summer, we were kept inside during the dark winter months. The shadow of the Moors Murders loomed large in the 1970s and parents had a visceral fear of 'Stranger Danger.' Time spent with parents and siblings indoors felt like time served at Her Majesty's pleasure, and 1970s parents did not to take prisoners when it came to discipline, my parents being no exception. The period from November to March was often profoundly depressing.

Like most parents of their generation, my parents were young when they had me, my older brother and younger sister. My dad was twenty-four when I was born and my mum twenty-six. Lots of energy and power, less wisdom and perspective, perhaps. Looking back, there was a vivid colour to the 1970s that contrasts sharply with the era of the two World Wars, and also seems far nicer than the grimy misery of the

1980s. My dad's dad was a soldier in World War Two, his grandad a soldier in World War One. There was a quasi-military feel to the winter months in our house, young soldiers confined to barracks, a place for everything and everything in its place. My dad is, without doubt, the single most contrary individual I have ever known; quite possibly the only person to enter the Royal Navy holding right-wing beliefs, reading Aryn Rand, yet leaving the Navy left-wing, reading Karl Marx. My late Mum was a proud Scouser, raised in Walton, in the shadows of Anfield and Goodison. Like me, Mum was the middle one (of five); like me, Mum had the capacity to cause an argument in an empty room and would not have prospered working in the diplomatic service. Mum was a nurse all her working life and took no shit from anyone. My Mum attributed this feistiness to having to toughen up when she became a nurse, although her younger brother, Michael, says Mum was plenty feisty before she started needing to work.

Dad is, to this day, a confirmed atheist; Mum was raised as a Catholic, and by dint of being a nurse, was well connected with the local Catholic mafia. We were all baptised as Catholics, then left to our own spiritual devices. Both sides of my family had strong Irish roots and I would describe my upbringing as culturally Catholic, although any faith I had died alongside my mum when she passed away from cancer at the age of fifty-five. Both my parents were smart, and they could see the way the wind was blowing after Thatcher won the 1979 General election; old industrial, working class jobs were disappearing for good. The election of 1979 was very much a crossing of the Rubicon; the UK ditched its industrial heritage, some would argue threw the working class under the bus, then vilified them for good measure.

The 1980s was a raw, turbulent decade; the Cold War was experiencing a terrifying renaissance, class war was being fought in the streets of Britain and sectarian conflict spilt over to mainland Britain from Northern Ireland. In 1981 there were race riots in Liverpool, London, Manchester and Birmingham, and anyone going to high profile football games were literally taking their life into their own hands, a state of affairs all too tragically exemplified by the numerous footballing tragedies of 1985. Out of this anger and hostility came a tsunami of cultural expression, the power of the sung and spoken word articulating the fury of social dislocation felt across Britain. From the poetry of The Salford Bard, John Cooper Clark, to the paired back resentment of The Specials' haunting 'Ghost Town', the de-industrialisation of the UK in the 1980s paradoxically proved a breeding ground for vibrant culture. Looking back, life in Manchester in the 1980s was wonderfully dangerous; watching matches at Old Trafford or Maine Road, going to concerts at The Apollo or The International, it all had an edge to it, rooted in the undeclared class war of that period. Punk played out next to Indie, Heavy Metal next to Ska, and all of it on show every Saturday in Manchester's effortlessly cool Underground Market.

In the summer of 1984, sixteen years of age, I sat my long-dreaded O-Levels, which went surprisingly well; in September 1984 I started my A-Levels and, for the first time, entered a far more middle class world. After our O-Levels, half of my mates stayed on at Sixth Form whilst the other half of my mates got jobs. Some of the lads who got jobs, I have never seen again. I was moving into far less familiar, far less comfortable territory, the girls I was seeing were suddenly middle class, well-spoken, well educated, had dads who were CEOs and drove Rovers or BMWs. The better I did in my A-Levels, the more one significant part of me felt like a class traitor. Being academically successful and working class felt like having my feet in two opposing camps, it felt wrong. Unlike many in my family, I was not blessed with practical abilities, although I was ok with words. To be honest, I felt unworthy and sometimes still do. These poems are, in part, a reflection on the cognitive dissonance I experienced during this period.

I spent four years gaining an American Studies degree from the University of Birmingham, with my third year based at the University of California, Berkeley. The three years spent at Birmingham were uniformly awful; Birmingham Uni was an Oxbridge overspill estate, populated by Barbour-wearing escapees from The Cotswolds. I hadn't grown up in poverty, materially or in terms of aspiration, but I had grown up working class, and at Birmingham the full enormity of Britain's unofficial caste system hit me. What use did I have for End-of-Year balls, hired tuxedos and cummerbunds? Genuinely awful upper-class cosplay.

The only time I ever fully felt comfortable in Brum was the time I spent working behind the bar at King's Head in Bearwood, at the junction of Lordswood and the Hagley Road. Solid people getting drunk in a normal way.

Then Berkeley happened, and everything changed. The year I spent studying in California was brilliant and life changing. It was liberating to live in an environment where everyone wore the same uniform of tee shirt and shorts, where no two people had the same accent, therefore no inferences could be made about people's character based on how they pronounced their words. Men and women played football then had civilised drinks after; the bars weren't full of drunken Rugby Union players daring each other to drink vomit and insert carrots into various orifices. Six thousand miles from Manchester, I felt like I'd come home. Most of all, the lecturers were hugely inspirational. I was fortunate enough to study under both Lawrence Levine and Earl Lewis at Berkeley, two heavyweights of learning who understood that, despite their brilliance, they couldn't just dial it in. Their lectures on American history and African-American studies were a masterclass in academic engagement, and were a huge influence on how I work with pupils and students to this day.

Every country has its own unique caste system, every caste system has its own specific shibboleths. Invisible barriers that hinder true social mobility; barriers all too apparent to those on the wrong side of the divide, and all too quickly excused, diminished or denied by those fortunate enough to be born on the right side. It's gaslighting on a national scale. In the UK, the caste system is class, reinforced by systems of education, justice and political power. In the US, the caste system is race, with a particular focus on Black Americans, reinforced by the same systems as the UK. Studying in the US freed me from the invisible guide rails of the British class system, yet I was fascinated by how the same process played out with different groups of society in the US. The books I read at Berkeley left an indelible mark on me: Claude Brown's *Manchild in the Promised Land*, Richard Wright's *Native Son*, his powerful haikus and the unfolding horror of Wright's stunning poem, *Between the World and Me*. The anger and beautiful clarity of the poems of Langston Hughes, for example *Dreams*, and Ralph Ellison's bleak existential novel, *Invisible Man*. This literature spoke to me on a visceral level in a way that European literature didn't and has certainly influenced poems within this book. My brother and I grew up on an entirely white estate as kids, yet *Manchild in the Promised Land* resonated with us both quite profoundly; perhaps because ultimately, it's a story of redemption.

After graduating in 1990, I briefly worked for Shell Oils, knocked that on the head, travelled in the USA and Australia before deciding to train as a teacher. I had wanted to be a teacher from the age of fifteen, but for a long time could not see a route through to achieving this. I vividly remember standing at the bottom of Schools Hill in Cheadle, at the end of another morning's paper round, reflecting on what seemed an unbridgeable gap between my ambition and my reality. Very few people I knew went to university, there was no discernible path to follow. I also very clearly recall walking to Parrs Wood School in Didsbury during my first teacher placement, extremely nervous about teaching my first solo lesson to a group of Year 10s. The lesson was on the causes of the Great Depression, and I started by playing Springsteen's *Johnny 99*. What if I was shit? What if I couldn't control a class? What if I was just plain dull? Fortunately, I was none of those things and had instead stumbled upon the one environment in my life where I feel entirely at ease, the classroom. I love teaching; love the energy, humour, drama, brutal honesty and level of challenge; standing alone in a room with thirty kids who owe you nothing.

Sadly, in my second year of teaching, in 1997, my mum passed away after a year battling lung cancer. Mum was fifty-five, my age now, and her death broke my heart and very nearly broke me as a person. The trauma of my late mum's illness, along with her eventual passing, were profoundly debilitating and took a lot of therapy and recovering from. One thing I have learnt over the years, however, is that life has a funny way of balancing things out. Five years after my Mum passed away, I plucked up the courage to ask out the most beautiful colleague I worked with - I was definitely 'punching' and (foolishly, perhaps) Nic said 'yes.' Six years later our wonderful son, Con, was born, and life took on a whole new meaning and purpose, as well as getting a whole lot more chaotic! The two poems at the centre of this book, *Son and heir*, and *You are here*, are dedicated to my beautiful, amazing wife and my wonderful, hilarious son.

Before Covid, I had toyed with the idea of finishing teaching at fifty-five, taking my pension and enjoying a life beyond work that my mum was never able to enjoy. In the event, Covid made that choice a necessity. Teaching during covid was brutal; having to quickly learn new, remote methods of teaching during lockdown, then stepping into the closely regulated classroom in the Autumn of 2020, knowing that if I caught Covid in my early fifties, the virus could kill me. During that autumn term of 2020, I had a conversation with a Year 8 lad in my Form, discussing the relative health risk we faced, and the necessity of teachers working in school rather than remotely. "After all," the young man said, "you've had your childhood..." He was 100% correct, it was right and proper that people of my generation risked their lives for the long-term wellbeing of kids, but that didn't make the endeavour any less scary. Exams were (rightly) cancelled and like a great many colleagues, I spent the time from Easter to Summer 2021 knee-deep in marking. By the end of July 2021, I was burnt out, had nothing more to give. One piece of advice I remember the late Lawrence Levine giving us in a lecture, was that "you have to know when to pick a book up, and it's just as important to know when to put a book down."

In July 2022, I resigned from teaching and decided to focus on writing this book of poems. September 2022 was the first September I hadn't worked since 1989, and it has been a pleasure and an immense privilege to walk our two dogs (Dexter and Duggie) over the hills of Delph as summer faded into Autumn, observing how the landscape around me changed as the weeks and months rolled by. These fifty-five poems therefore cover a variety of themes important to me, such as teaching, nature, trauma, love and place. The more I wrote, the more I realised that an over-arching theme was the way in which individual lives are corralled by lines and boundaries, often invisible. These are often arbitrary social constructs, caste systems in effect, sometimes reinforced by geographical boundaries. Despite a lot of subtle, and not so subtle pressure to stay in our respective lanes, the real challenges and best adventures in life are to be found by crossing these lines. Some of my poems are political, although this is not an overtly political book. I do despair about some aspects of the UK, post-pandemic, and it would be wrong not to articulate that concern. At the same time, I think that we sixty-seven million Brits live in a beautiful country, and that the overwhelming majority of us are kind, decent people. Certainly, my experience as a teacher of almost thirty years has been that all but a handful of pupils, I have met have been good 'uns, even if that is buried a bit deeper in some than others. I could have included twice the number of poems that I have in these pages, however one of the most important themes in this book is age, influenced by the young age that my mum passed away. I feel I am only just getting my head around the complexities of life as I hit fifty-five, and it saddens me greatly that I never got to know my mum when we were both fully formed adults. It is tremendously that Nic and Con never got to know my mum; she was a force of nature. For this reason, I have included just fifty-five poems in this collection.

So, yes, there is sadness within some of these poems, but this is not a sad book; I have loved walking, observing, reflecting, writing and refining over the past six months. I tend to write my poems on my phone; I will be out and about, and a phrase will pop into my head. From that one phrase, two or three words, I have a focus from my poem, and will slowly work through the structure, more often than not whilst I am still out with the dogs. When I get home, I'll type up the poem on my phone, email it to my personal email, then edit my writing. I like the immediacy and simplicity of writing poems this way, it has a clarity to it that works for me. I am fifty-five next month, finally able to apply for my Teacher's pension, and writing this book is a way of celebrating this milestone, as well as commemorating my Mum's life, a life that was cruelly cut short. I hope you enjoy reading these poems as much as I have enjoyed writing them.

Cheers,

Tony

A580 - (East Lancs Road)

I span the East Lancs,
Kingsway to Queens Drive,
70s Pier Head to
the source of the Mersey.
Irish humour; no mercy.

Tenant farm to council house,
half Manc, half Scouse.
One foot in each camp
astride the East Lancs.
All routes lead back to Ireland,
Tipperary and Wicklow.

Descended, as a great man once said,
from immigrants and revolutionists.
From the docks to the runway,
hospital wards to the classroom,
Unionised and proud, hard work a given,
"no one owes you a living."

"You'll never sign-on in this house, lad."

Matriarchs and patriarchs,

hewn from granite,

iron fists in spiked gloves.

There was love, but it was tough,

at either end of the East Lancs.

Snow Line

Above the snow line,

deer tracks run to the quarry.

Dogs dance in the snow.

Below the snow line,

bin truck collects detritus.

Winter bisects Delph.

Across the snow line,

Fox treads warily, silent.

Out on manouevres.

No worries

In the pre-adolescent mind's eye, the
Micker Brook unfolded like the mighty
Mississippi.

Empty barrels lashed onto pilfered
pallets, using ropes Ross Ray stole.

Swing over water, leap on, twist off, bang!

Ferrying passengers back from the other side,

red brick wall with 'Kinny Was Ere' painted on.

Get wet, get bollocked.

Punk; an explosion of lascivious intent,

nine years old getting our heads around *Friggin
in the Rigging*. Unsure of either end of the
rhyme.

Papers full of Johnny Rotten, silver jubilee, God
Save the Queen.

The Fascist regime. Drying off jeans in the
summer sun.

In early autumn we'd raid apples from the
clinic orchard,

play split the kipper, flying flick knives, hunt
for conkers and light a new fire.

Everybody got injured and nobody moaned.

Dazzler with his compound fracture,

Ant McFinn broke his collarbone hurtling off a
railway embankment rope swing; rest of us
collapsed laughing.

Stockport infirmary took us all in,

patched us up; X ray, local

anaesthetic, tetanus shot, stitches.

Badges of honour, then home on the bus.

Bar-rie, Curbie,

kick-stone and Wembley.

Gordon is a Moron and Botham heroics.

Gary swinging golf clubs, Lez smoking stubs.

Cricket wicket painted on the rec,

Arnie with wickets, pads and bat,

Shorty striding in, corkie exploding from his
freckled fingers, implausible speed.

No helmet.

No gloves.

No worries.

Town

Train rolls slowly into Piccadilly,
back to our city.
Industrial side streets,
newly opened bars,
fresh faced students mingle
with mid nineties veterans.
Newbies and scallies embrace
the same vibrant energy.

Pedestrianised roads fight
for attention whilst children of
Lowry stumble drunkenly down
Tib Street. Every evening framed
in Mancunian noir. Drizzle-grey
skies warn of imminent soaking.
Orange street lights reflect back from
semi-permanent puddles.

Footie fans and Saturday

afternoon shoppers make

their retreat; new troops arrive

at the front line, spilling boisterously

out of buses and trams.

Girls and boys glammed up and ready;

station bounces with the possibilities

of fresh adventures.

A seedy undercurrent keeps the

evening on its toes; drug dealers and

prostitutes circle just beyond the shine

of the concourse. Men and women dressed like
teenagers:

hoodies and trackies; drawn faces and hopeless
eyes speak of a harsher night for some.

Chasing what passes for the sun in the early
hours.

New buildings, fresh faces, cycle shops

where garment factories used to be;

Cobbled streets at the foot of half-finished
skyscrapers,

red lights and cranes occupy the eye line,
dominate the skyline.

The city grows up and out,

but the old pubs still groan with crowded bars,

scars of the pandemic healing over.

8th Street

J et-lag internal balaclava,

circadian rhythm on catch-up,

I walk west 100 yards down 8th Street,

morning sun on my back. Scramble

down the dusty embankment, storm

drain. LA bound train hurtles past,

double-deckered silver blur.

No functioning fence, instead a

childlike sense of adventure, dart

across the single rail track.

Climb warily up the steep path,

stand on top of a crumbling cliff,

long disused routes down to the beach.

Here, on this precise spot, at this

precise time, standing on the very edge

of a vast continent. Mind blown.

Battery Park a long way east,

Bruntwood Park even further.

Below, men my age balance

precariously on thin carbon boards,

some solitary, others in pairs,

steeling themselves for the next wave,

next day in the office. Lone board

breaks ranks, carries its nonchalant

 passenger back to shore. A scene both

mesmerising and barely

comprehensible, six thousand miles

from my usual breakfast routine.

In the evening I repeat my pilgrimage,

feel the last of the day's warmth on my

face, watching the sun dip lazily beyond

the Pacific horizon, beyond Midway,
welcoming in a cool Japanese morning.

Here, poised on this crumbling

precipice, edge of the notional 'West.'

Vast ocean reaches to the earth's curve,

humbling privilege to return again.

Nah

Neither Protestant work ethic, nor
Catholic guilt, can shift me out
from below my quilt.

Old friends, colleagues, at 9 am

brave Monday morning email

hell. Not me.

Rain hasn't stopped, not a moment's

rest; all things considered and knowing

what's best, I'll slumber on.

September

Septembet rolls harmlessly by,
across the West Riding of Yorkshire,
depleted reservoirs glisten below;
lilac heather hangs off Dark Peak,
languid, shorn of malice.

Moors are dry,
across which long shadows
of occasional clouds are cast.
Sky Road home,
shimmering bikes emerge,
flash passed,
fade to the east.

There are vineyards now;
hope, trust in
this unknown future.
Manchester emerges over the horizon,
west coast promise beyond Mancunian grime.

Far off, Fiddlers Ferry;

stark, devoid of charm,

anachronistic even.

Beyond which,

Silhouette of Welsh mountains reflects back a lifetime.

The late summer sky bleeds into a golden fireball,

sun sets way across Cheshire.

Chlorophyll molecules cling valiantly on,

resisting the approaching cool of autumn.

This month I have not witnessed before;

stumbled past it, anxious, intimidated.

in fear of another academic year.

There is a mature beauty here,

understated nobility,

English countryside at its proudest,

this summer meanders, no arbitrary deadlines,

it will fade as it should:

In timely fashion, with good grace.

Identity

Who am I right now?
Enfant retiree, or one
more burnt out teacher?

Look up

Sun hangs low over
midwinter Hills.
Wet concrete and yesterday's
grit underfoot.

Look up.

See blurred branches

in skeletal trees.

Kids pass by,

weighed down by a term's

relentless grind.

Huddled in bus stops.

Look up.

See Mars flirt with the moon,

above Orion's gaze.

Fields lose their lustre,

Winter silences nature's voice.

There are grey days when the sun

misses its appointment.

Look up.

See silhouetted ears

of a nervous deer.

Fields and windows frozen,

clear across the valley.

Football pitches silent, abandoned

for what remains of this year.

Look up.

See a solitary Kestrel

hover with intent.

The Tyre place

Great people,
Good poh-leece
(as they say on The Wire).

Puce face,

thinning hair,

radio blasting.

And the fellas there know every

single word.

Dean Moriarty;

throwing rubber,

talking shite.

"'Kin hell, Ant,

You are one fat bastard!."

Hooded ghosts stumble past,

intersection between mill town and present.

Vape rises from this valley

of decency and crime.

Metro trundles past in the

shadow of victorian ghosts.

Red brick Cathedral reaches into

a slate grey sky.

Once, we were everything.

We readjust,

take stock.

Evolve.

Metro tracks across Victorian

railways;

echoes of a distant era,

no nearer as a nation

to appreciating

the essential labour of our working classes.

Pandemic!

P andemic!
Can't help but remind me,
David Simon's Baltimore.

Public health catastrophe,

heralded by the poor

in this broken town;

terraced death traps,

pitiless poverty.

A remote, dissembling source

of chaotic decision making fills

the funeral parlours;

one growth industry amidst

furloughed futures.

Invite only at the local Crems.

Weddings,

Christenings,

Sacraments on hold.

All hope paused,

Bubbles shuffles forward,

masked,

forlorn,

Pandemic panic in a

patient British queue.

The dead brought out

On wheelchairs,

final words wattsapped to

helpless loved ones.

Ventilator roulette.

Hotline

I am poised.
I am ready.
I am alert.

Yet powerless.

I am informed

I am poised,

alert.

Agile.

Watching.

I am ready,

poised,

knowledgeable,

I have no agency.

I read,

watch,

listen,

I keep up.

My voice is irrelevant.

Ready,

poised,

astute

Have sense that is common and not.

I wait.

I am anxious,

avaricious in my quest for the latest

information.

For all the good it does me.

I sit.

I read.

Scroll,

rage.

Repeat.

My hotline is unused.

Kids today

As kids we could be vile.

Two bachelors lived in a
dilapidated house on our estate;

Blackjack and Ernie.

"Blackjack is a fat twat" we would scrawl,

stone in hand, across pavement,

in front of their bedraggled curtains.

Then wipe the bile off,

play hopscotch,

Kick-can.

A classmate, James, ghostly white,

lost in a world of autism we had no
understanding of.

We never teased James,

different story with his mum.

"Jesus is in my heart" she would tell us,

frightened Scottish brogue,

moving warily past us.

"Jesus is in your hat?" we would taunt.

Remorseless,

devoid of empathy,

revelling in our cruelty.

On our estates, the vulnerable were mocked,

windows were smashed,

houses and cars alike.

Shops were robbed,

so too the Smiths Crisps factory

In Cheadle Heath;

small kids,

large boxes,

trophies carried ostentatiously home,

distributed down by the rope swing.

So let's not hear about "kids today."

Nothing

What happens if I do nothing?
Could I simply stop, cease and desist?

This raises the question of what "something" is; relative merit attributed to arbitrary actions.

Is being a dad not enough?

Driving my wonderful son to school,

picking him up at the end of

another long day; walking the dogs up

on the deserted moors.

Why do I feel a level of guilt when

people ask if I am bored yet?

Of what? Of whom?

I was very bored of endless meeting,

pointless politics.

Does the habit of wanting my ducks in a

row achieve anything other than

creating senseless order at the expense

of spontaneity, or creativity.

Should I blast those ducks clear out of the sky?

And this? Something? Nothing?

Do I have to monetise these thoughts to

bestow worth upon them? As my mate

Malc always says, we get institutionalised.
Invisible chains.

Room to breathe

Slouch,

cower,

atrophy.

Scheme;

perhaps die.

Escape route planned,

this suffocating childhood

cannot stand.

Slow Sunday purgatory,

Roast spuds,

soulless ritual,

life-stifling rigour mortis.

All these years later,

I sometimes struggle in the evening.

Tonight, however, the full moon casts

shadows; foxes tread lightly,

five deer, near, shelter.

Dex and Dugs sniff, bark, agitate.

I sleep soundly,

house at peace.

The Crossing

In dinghies, trucks,
airline undercarriage,
trying their luck.

Not to scrounge,

take and lounge,

they head to our shores,

want to explore

the 'Great' in our name.

From the Sahel they endure,

to experience our fame;

our kindness,

compassion,

welcoming spirit.

Still here.

Of a fashion.

It's happened before,

boats on our shore,

Belgians in 1914,

European Jews in the 30s

Daily Hate even then sharing

Its dirty secret:

racist bile,

'No Blacks

Dogs

Irish.'

Nothing new here,

same suspicion and fear,

Powellite playbook

to adhere to.

But hey,

This was my family too,

made me,

made you.

From Clonmel and Wicklow,

Ukraine,

Beyond.

Us,

Me,

You,

together.

The 'Great' in this Britain,

and if you love your footie

Then yes,

You'll fit in.

Hint of Autumn

As summer wanes, hint of autumn caught on the tail of a September breeze.

Sky remains blue, flowers persist, although

their beauty fades, vibrancy dissipates.

Leaves beginning to turn, lose

their grip; sycamore seeds scatter.

Back to Work

L ilac harbinger,
sad end to six weeks' respite.
Forlorn, back we trudge.

Polite Thuggery

The polite thuggery of the
English ruling class;
kill, starve,

freeze, drown,

by all means.

But please, no swearing, and

try not to raise your voice.

Yes, of course, go ahead:

steal, defraud,

dissemble, gaslight,

pilfer and bully.

Fill your pockets and boots.

However, let's not use the word 'lie',

shall we? Such an ugly word.

Heavy shoes

These heavy shoes drag wearily up
disused railways; along back lanes,
frenzy of summer has retreated,
alone,

I am treated to an early autumn blaze of sun.

Beside the canal towpath, ducks cackle

at some obscure joke; English reserve

on display. A curt nod, a whispered "hello."

Above, pensionable sunlight falls

defiantly onto a still-green canopy,

thinning like an old man's hair.

Tired leaves fall onto refurbished industrial
routes.

Incomprehensible to me that in a few

short weeks these trees will have lost

their last; single track railway open to

raw winter.

At Measurements I switch track,

steep uphill. I emerge, Knarr Mill, knackered.

At home the dogs sleep, waiting for my final
ascent up the Brun Lee.

The Wrong Season

L ate May again,
    same child-part of me
    dies; local council makes its
seasonal culling

In a run-down gym

desks set out, meticulous

precision; few hundred more

feed the meat grinder.

Generation upon generation

searching for answers in the dull

noon heat: where have all the

goal posts gone?

Off-kilter

Tiny silver tear in the pastel sky,
a millimetre fuselage, mirage,jets
east. Disrobed trees offer up
abandoned nests in the silent
afternoon. Across darkening fields
sheep wander in formation,
devouring the winter yield.

.

On the TV, in stark contrast, a carnival
of ghouls plays out, common decency
on hold as the 'ballet of the masses'
abandons all pretence of compassion.
The weather is unusually mild,
summertime sport an incongruous
harbinger of Christmas.

On winter pathways, carpeted with
abandoned leaves, a solitary wimberry

bush holds forth an implausible harvest,

whilst T-shirted neighbours decorate

their outdoor Christmas trees in the late

afternoon warmth. Off-kilter winter

messes with my mind.

Berkeley

California was further then,
alone on the Hayward fault.
Phone calls a rarity; long-penned
letters, transcontinental,

trans-Atlantic.

Driving past the outrageous beauty of

night-time San Francisco,

or to feel the rumble of Bay Bridge concrete,

Friday evening, off into the city.

A year of living freely, untethered from trauma,

12 months of vivid spring.

Sunsets over thinly drawn Golden Gate,

weekend footie in the vast Cal arena.

A riot of early 20s adventure,

Sunday 6am BART back to Berkeley.

Late night naked shenanigans

down mercifully deserted I House corridors.

On a glorious spring morning we drove,

pre-dawn, to the Sierra Nevada mountains;

stood on pristine snow,

staring over to the bleak Nevada desert.

The next day we dug our car out of

4 am snow fall, began the winding drive

back to the Bay area.

That evening, we played footie in 35 degree heat.

For that one year, Autumn was cancelled;

trees remained clothed

in vibrant colours. No West Midlands misery,

sodden bus stops, 4pm evenings.

Rock star University lecturers,

humble, brilliant, unaffected. Earl Lewis

Introducing me to the heroes of the

Harlem Renaissance; poetry of Langston
Huges.

To travel six thousand miles and find peace,

this manchild in the promised land,

 weightless living, far from the oppressive

shadow of 80s England.

Pros and Cons

Free for an evening;
trapped tomorrow. Dull grey fog
clouds hungover soul.

Dinas Dinlle

There is a beach, south of Caernarfon,

quiet, unassuming, the first beach I
fell in love with.

Twice a year our grandparents,

Walter and Molly, would take us caravanning
in North Wales, edge of Snowdonia.

The excitement I felt as we drove through
Betws-Y-Coed,

past the ugly house, then flew through

the Llanberis Pass, was palpable.

Our Grandad would drive us, shortcut,

through the back roads of Caernarfon,

heading to the beach at Dinas Dinlle.

Thin strip of sand, no shortage of rocks

with which we built beach dens, sat

contented in the evening sun.

Narrow country lanes, skin feeling tight with

the sun's afterglow, laughing as we

waited our turn to pass on tight roads.

There are more beautiful beaches on the

Lleyn Peninsula, no doubt,

yet none more evocative for me.

Pre-teen moment in time, innocence,

excitement, adventure; scrambling up

the nearby cliff face.

An old World War Two Seagull Trench

piqued our curiosity, spoke of the war

a generation or so before.

Grandad telling us about his dad's

Boer War tall stories and actual exploits on

the Battlefields of Belgium.

Visceral connection to events impossible

to imagine in the late afternoon

1970s sun. Harder still now.

Time

Time does not heal,
though it does add perspective.
Opportunities to build again,
reconstruct a shattered heart.

That hole in your life,

it never closes over;

just looks smaller the more you

move away from the trauma.

The memories of our loved ones

are our loved ones, they never fade.

How could they? Other beautiful

vistas distract and engage us.

Bitter sweet recollection of an adored

parent swim alongside the recent delight

of fist-bumping your four-year

old neighbour. Life moves on.

Son and heir

You,

fireball of energy,

infinite heart.

Unstoppable bundle of love,

fount of all hilarity.

Gentle soul, biting humour.

Kickabout kid;

sweet left foot,

Brexit tackles.

Kindness and compassion

expressed in the language of a

docker; precocious student

of Anglo Saxon.

Know this:

there is not one part of you

I would ever swap.

I love you more than

more than everything

You are here

You are here, on these battlements:
life plays out far below, hint of
autumn carried on the air.
You are here, beside me, laughing.

Picasso print on new walls,
dogs asleep on their quilts,
standing here on our terrace,
You are here, beside me, planning.

The two of us sat out, listening,
Owls chatting, stream dancing.
Tonight the planets are exiled,
You are here, perpetual motion.

Quicksilver

B ifolds open,
dawn chorus;
merest hint of spring as a
distant owl bids adieu.
Quicksilver planet hovers, south,
chameleon sky.

The dogs bark at an unseen foe,
camouflaged eyes.
High above, white-streak jet,
unwavering, east, towards
the awakening sun.

A morning so still, Castleshaw disappears
into its own reflection.
To the west, white blob bobtail
Roe deer stands,
quick scan across the hills,
disappears across frozen fields.

Oblivious

Bars so finely crafted, they
disappear into the azure sky.
A cage so devilishly devised,
or so Marx surmised.
Free to roam, explore,
cross borders and boundaries;
impossible to leave.
Capitalist exile,
priced per the mile,
oblivious, we smile.

Greed hardwired into us,
no simple clothes,
nor crown of thorns.
Cognitive dissonance on an
Industrial scale.
Our greatest suffering woven
into the lies we tell ourselves.
The money-lender's table rebuilt,

re-fitted, dull witted we stumble,

ceaseless fingers fumble for the

plastic card entrapemnt.

We, bovine masses, mired

in our own denial, and all the while,

on Wall Street, The Square Mile,

vultures circle, smile.

Bars so exquisitely crafted,

an iron cage in a velvet glove.

Ghosts

Ghosts of late childhood
haunt my dreams on sober nights,
of no consequence.

Beyond the harbour,

mountainous seas capsize our

flimsy vessel, Youth.

Infinite ocean,

time, protects the dignity of

foolish younger selves.

Soldier

Bent double,
dead weight rucksack
bites at her young shoulders.
Snorkel jacket shut tight,

impervious:

to February frost,

mindless misogyny,

Tiktok scrutiny.

Resolute stroll across dawn-quiet

No-man's land,

back pitch.

Destination, English.

Weighed down by the

existential suffering of

 dead white men,

canon fodder.

The post-covid wave march forward;

A third mowed down,

failed by examination.

One war actually won on

the playing fields of Eton.

Onwards, ever onwards.

River of Mist

River of mist meanders, south.
Through to Chew Valley.
Mill village shrouded
in cotton cloud.

The morning churn of commuter traffic
grumbles west: purgatory for the
digital age, souls trapped
in an invisible cage.

Below the moon, straight-line
vapour trail underlines the ambiguity
of this moment. Long shadows cast as
the dogs and I head home.

Pony

Miniature pony
grazes on old Roman road:
dusk falls over Delph.

Bypass

The freedom of my youth has
been bypassed every which way.
Fields that I sledded down in
rare winter snow have been concreted
over. The changing rooms I
prepared for matches in have
been replaced by John Lewis fitting
rooms; the ref swapped for an
attendant, designer suits
instead of footie kits.

The long summer grass I waded through
one night, Springsteen blaring, more
than a little drunk, has long since gone,
instead a petrol station looms large.
Country lanes I felt safe running down
are now racing circuits for just-passed
teenagers and homeward-bound

Premier League players; fastest route to
Bowden.

The five straight roads I could cycle

down to watch the planes land at the

end of Shadowmoss Lane are now a

blurred complexity of hotels, tramlines

and 24/7 traffic. No shortcut through to

Mobberley available behind Ringway.

Fields of dreams tarmaced over with a

second runway.

Subterranean nightclubs slung along

the A34 are long gone, so too the

down-at-heel hotels they resided under.

The long walk home, Gus hobbling on

crutches, has disappeared amidst a

plethora of newly built housing estates and

roundabouts. There was a moment, it was
perfect, and now it's all demolished. That's how
the cookie crumbles.

As of yet, however, there are no plans to

demolish, replace or concrete over the

Indelible memories of our collective late

teens; scenes of excitable joy and

drunken heartache. Pre-exam parties

and results-day piss-ups. Perched as I am,

high in the Saddleworth hills, in love,

surrounded by family, it's a wonderful
privilege to be able to look across at the neon
colour of

Yesterday, and smile.

An eye

Venn diagram existence,

my life,

misery of others,

our suffering.

To what extent is my

suffering vicarious guilt?

Appropriating pain for

personal gain.

The more I focus on the Right,

the less I care about what's left.

The territory I survey is greater

than this thumb-print obsession;

touch-screen poverty tourism.

Portrayed as heroes or villain,

in the centre, an eye, connecting.

Nexus of guilt and judgement.

I have wasted far too much time

pondering the complexity of

Life around me.

Crossroad

Back at this crossroad I
recall from my youth.
Roads were quieter,
yet the weight presses lighter now.

Traffic is busier,

more people travelling these roads.

I'll approach with customary caution,

eyes open, less to hide.

Dark reaches of a previous life

exposed to the cleansing light of love.

Once more there are avenues to explore,

although the stakes are not so high now;

wisdom of a million mistakes to fall back on.

Leave nobody behind.

Gazing down at the crossroad from

these hills, my vantage point,

horizon stretches far beyond

the hopes of my childhood.

So: quick swig of tea,

demolish an orange slice or two,

blast of my inhaler, check

my laces, ready for the second half.

Fifty Five not out.

Fifty five not out,
carried my bat until tea;
tough session ahead.

Martyrs

Neither Erasmus nor I
are the stuff of martyrs.
Neither sweet nor proper to perish
in this meat grinder.

Fuck that for a game of soldiers.
Jan Huss, Thomas Cranmer,
Latimer and Ridley,
You guys took one hell of a beating.

The game is the game

The loop is closed, shut off to new ideas.
The system works: one third are
sacrificed,
no riddle to solve, no puzzle to triumph over.

Each year offers tired solutions, endless series
of improbable theories regurgitated. Truth is,
if it ain't broke, you can't fix it.

New recruits are awed into compliance as the
mid-Thirties gang,
with religious zeal, try to invigorate, initiate,
overcome.
Neither cohort able to grasp the full picture.

The game is the game, and worth playing. profit
margins are slim, hard work is not met with
requisite reward, yet still we fight on.

Defender of the Faith.

Familiar template, defender of the faith.
The cast our own sorrow onto her,
the slenderest of broad shoulders.

Hands bruised, skin tracing-paper thin,
all of us familiar with the frail matriarch;
our own beloved grandparents.

Across these four divided nations, we
pause for silent reflection, united by
our common loss.

The Border

Knott Hill, sunrise;
biting easterly wind sends
white horses careering across
Castleshaw.

Fields below on fire with Willowherb,
trees down in the village ablaze with
the ravages of late October.

Stiff breeze from across the Pennines brings
the threat of an Arctic winter,
heather rusts as the seasons turn.

Clocks

Spring forward,
fall backwards, into a
dark and damp British
November. The UK stripped
of high-sun beauty. We remember
Celtic Samhain and uncovered plots.

On the bonfire, Guido burns again;
Penny for the Guy sadly retired.
Mischief Night a wry smile
memory; old traditions
replaced as cruel
winter prevails.

Barcheston Avenue

I n a more simple time, before
CCTV, outdoor light sensors,
I Phones, FIFA or PS4,
as the nights drew in,
with great alacrity and much hilarity,
hedges were hopped,
fences were hurdled.

Where Barcheston met Broadway,
the team would assemble, nervous
for the night's excitement.
Misty autumn evenings, run up to
Bonfire night, time for mischief.
Routes planned, watches synchronised.
Suburban steeplechase
through the leafy back
gardens of South Manchester.

A silent procession, whispered

warnings, hush-toned instructions.

Cheadle's very own Ho Chi Minh

Trail. Leave no friend behind and

watch out for the Alsation at Number 7.

Outdoor furniture and climbing

frames tastefully rearranged. Or

swapped with a neighbour. We won't mention

the space hopper; what happens on tour

Stays on tour.

Unspoken rules; you get caught

you get battered. No parents or

police. No names, no pack drill.

Thrill of the chase, running never easy

with a belly full of laughter. More

than able to outpace the incandescent

 beer grifter. At the end of the evening,

we would drift away, talking up the near

misses, comparing our injuries.

Planning the next night.

Hope

These jaded satellite towns,
mills derelict or re-purposed,
soulless service sector businesses.

Where once there was
skilled weekly work; footie on a
Saturday, faith on a Sunday.
People adrift in industrial decline.

Men fester, fume, bound tight by
stereotypes forged in the blast furnaces
of the abandoned steel works, Brexit
generation at breaking point.

Meanwhile, hospital visits are invasive,
unwanted, open gowns, doctors frown
guiding cameras where the sun don't
shine. Not all news benign.
Yet, hope stirs in the minds of some,

Mental health football, talking groups,

walking troops, where fellas can let go

of shared trauma.

For talk we men must, explore and expose

Our collective experience, refute the

dangerous lie: "men don't cry, stiff upper lip,

 crack on with it, kid."

Conversation a priceless prescription,

inoculate against self-imposed exile,

smile, have faith in the values and decency

of ourselves and our fellow man.

The need and the means

The need and the means,

This house of wisdom and pain,

childhood paradox.

Compassion

Anger cannot create compassion,
if your heart is an empty shell,
you are wasting your time
searching

for decency within.

Spleen vented is cool, cathartic,

for a short while, so smile,

dust yourself down, grow.

White hot rage won't move the soulless,

not one millimetre; empathy never arose

from the flames of furious indignation.

Cut them off, cross them out,

erase their relevance, influence on your life.

Leave them to their stone cold heart,

and smile.

The Deep South

Si, balls of steel.
drives this shitty car
from Long Island, through
downtown Manhattan, clear
to the New Jersey Turnpike.
In search of Langford, The Boss,
adventure and identity. January
storms left in our Mancunian wake.
Eastern seaboard, Atlanta bound, rocking
up at a tired Youth Hostel, quick unpack,
a serious thirst on, heading to the
nearest neon sign: "Buddies."
Puzzled by the frosty reception at the bar.
"Si, there are no women here…"
"Course there are, those over there…"
"Si, they're not women!"
No judgement on our part, just
the need for a drink.
"You guys lost?" the incandescent barman

asked, "You want a titty bar?"

Nope, just a beer and a game of pool.

Onwards to Athens, venturing through

the impoverished South, wrong

turns taking us deep into abject poverty,

arriving finally at Weaver Ds.

Fine food on East Broad Street,

service so good it's automatic for the people.

Stepping into the footsteps of legends at

The 40 Watt Club; T Shirts bought, photos

posed for, the night still young.

Excitement brought to an untimely end, kicked

out at midnight, to be met outside

by a queue to get back in; new cover charge, a
dry bar.

Dumbfounded, we crossed the street, sought

answers in a deserted diner: "the hell just
happened?" Si asked the pretty Southern girl
behind the counter.

"You're in the Deep South, honey…" the girl
laughed.

55

What would we say if we met?

How could we talk through the tears?

Decades without seeing each other;

me your son, you my mother,

Both of us 55.

How long would we have?

A day, or an hour, to explore

all the lost years, both of our fears,

of death, family, love.

Both 55.

At least I was lucky, said goodbye,

sat quietly adjacent as you escaped

12 months of pain. But where did you go?

How could you be gone?

Both 55.

Nobody knows when our last words are spoken, a last hug, the final kiss.

I'd settle for either, five minutes besides you.

Laugh, cry, a final goodbye.

Both of us 55.

Pop Van

The Pop Van would rock up when least expected,

money was tight, though, and most days 'Pop' of the

'Corporation' variety was the only one available.

Ice cream Pied Piper every Sunday, halfway through

ITV footie highlights; Gerald Sinstadt waxing lyrical

as West Brom tore Gary Bailey a new one.

No corner shops, no Sunday shopping; instead a dusty

1950s grocer's van would do the rounds. Cabbage

motorhome for the unprepared or infirm.

Every summer, maybe two, an unannounced,

seemingly endless stream of circus trucks

would light up a mundane weekend morning.

The rec across the road transformed, Big Top
thrown up,

me judged grown up enough to go and explore
the

mysteries of our temporary new neighbours.

Away for hours, lost in a fairytale world of
candyfloss

and elephant manure; our estate brought to life
by the

off-duty clowns, spitting llamas, ropes and
canvas.

Looking back, barely believable, the circus
seems

like a plotline from an Enid Blyton book,

So magical, fantastical, a distant memory by my
late teens.

Underground Market

Denim jackets, combats, leather,
bondage trousers held together by
bright elastic.

Josh sticks, incense, badges,

bootleg Bowie and snide recordings,

Ardwick's most recent offering.

Metal-heads, punks, the odd Mod,

wrist-bands, petunia oil.

New Romantic pleated kecks,

Vinyl, tapes, for the decks at home,

Bury, Broadbottom, Stockie, Oldham.

All roads leading to the sound,

smell, effortlessly cool energy; Saturday in

the underground market.

Ignore the rain above, football club in

the doldrums, soul sapping single-sex

education of those early years of

Thatcher. Here, walls exuded energy,

hope, identity.

Long gone now; alive only in the

YouTube explorations of urban

 explorers. But before Afflecks, before

gentrification, filing in from the stations,

Oxford Road, Victoria, swarm of

youth who knew the vibrancy of our city.

Sunlit Town

There are too many
people hurting in this
sunlit town.

Trapped between neon gloss
and the crushing weight of
a peripheral existence.

The little fellas help a little,
of a weekend, help
from an old friend.

Shifts are erratic, mundane,
lack of routine that remains the
same. In this sunlit town.

Come November, hope
hibernates, held in abeyance;
long wait for spring.

Friendships are tidal,
a questionable investment
in this transient predicament.

Possibilities recede, disappear,
kaleidoscope flashbacks,
hastily abandoned backpacks.

No permanence nor safety,
tossed around, flotsam and
jetsam, in this sunlit town.

Poacher turned gamekeeper

You can't kid a kidder, Mo, this is the
thing, so take out those earrings,
take off your ring.

Open your textbook, please, close up
your gob. Crack on with your work,
don't act like a knob.

It's not my first rodeo, Jess, not in the
slightest, that essay you wrote, by some
distance the shitest.

So pack away your death stare, save it
for later. Crack on with your work,
pen hitting paper.

I wasn't born yesterday, I'm as old as
the hills, more than prepared for this
battle of wills.

But I've been there myself, son, I know

how it feels, there's no judgement on

my part so let's strike a deal:

let's neither of us take the piss out the

other, I enjoy teaching you, you're just

like my brother.

Hold onto your feistiness, don't lose

your spirit, the game is the game and we both

need to win it.

The Universe and I

The universe and I are
OK.
For now,
ish.

kinda.

Tectonic turbulence becalmed,

smoothed over,

ironed out,

The universe and I are at peace;

Temporary truce.

Nothing holds,

this we know.

But for now we both rest,

wait,

prepare.

The universe and I remain vigilant.

Just

In

Case.

Events move quickly round here,

whilst simultaneously decaying

at a glacial space.

Atrophy sets in.

Apathy,

astonishingly enough.

The universe and I are at peace,

I am beginning to think that,

perhaps,

The universe is playing the long game.

Sneaky fucker.

Across the lines.

There are lines!

Are there lines?

Their lies hide and disguise,

that which is felt but not seen,

perspex screen.

Unwritten laws, unspoken codes,

arbitrary, carved out of thin air,

gossamer thin, wholly unyielding.

On these tribal shores, Freud's narcissism

of small differences prevails, rarely

fails in its designated purpose.

Freudian, feudal. To Eton the spoils,

middle classes fool themselves into

erroneous acceptance and the post war

council estates resonate with the

sound of managed decline.

Those who escape enter an alien world

of etiquette, Barbour, end of term balls,

adrift upon a suffocating Oxbridge

over-spill estate landscape.

There are lines.

Are there? lines?

Invisible to the immigrant's eye

on the 9th floor.

Visceral in the classroom, where

colonial prejudices ripple,

rotten stone tossed in a stagnant pond.

Eldest child stepping out onto

North-West streets, the stain of defeat has

etched borders unknown to the

uninitiated. Waited for hands

of warmth, acceptance. Too few came

and in the end cracked on, like her Mum

told her people do back home.

There are lines.

Are there though?

Politicians, writers, actors, cricketers,

attribute their success to natural

resilience, wit, intelligence.

Willfully unaware of the table, how it

tilts. Fee paying grammars, hammer

home privilege on an annual basis,

esteemed Uni places assigned

behind thick wooden doors,

Oak-paneled boardrooms,

war rooms, gaming this on-going class battle.

Gerrymandered bursaries, undeserved tax
breaks.

There are lines.

Not here? Where our better

angels fear to inspect too closely.

Abrahamic faiths dividing,

subdivisions, Protestant, Catholic,

Sunni, Shia, Orthodox, Liberal, Reform.

From Belfast to North Manchester,

Glasgow to the dilapidated Pennine Mill

towns. From the God without,

to God within

There are lines.

Are they white?

Alongside which, adults old enough to

know better still fight. And despise.

Industrial works team in a satellite age,

Rage spewing forth, the whole

length of the M62.

Colours, worn in pride hide self defeating
stupidity.

Tribal rigidity allowing the powers that be to

murder with impunity. Idiot fans sing of losses
that

are shared, too pissed up to see the oneness of
the crosses

these communities bear.

There are lines.

There *are* lines.

There.

Designed to divide, define;

malign intent. Spun in the finest gold,

Set in stone. Written down,

indelible; in languages dead and alive.

Snake oil misogyny, some might say.

It may well be that the best thing

we can do is to cross over, cross out,

erase, eradicate, challenge, step over,

stamp down on, antagonise and question

every single last line. All of them

man-made. Don't be afraid:

cross that line.